TUSCANY

PHOTOGRAPHS BY

SONJA BULLATY & ANGELO LOMEO

TEXT BY

MARIE-ANGE GUILLAUME

ABBEVILLE PRESS   PUBLISHERS

NEW YORK   LONDON   PARIS

*Front jacket and
pages 10–11.
cypresses
Val d'Orcia*

*Back jacket.
irises and grapevines
Poggio della Croce*

*Page 1.
roses in springtime
Regello*

*Pages 2–3.
avenue of trees
near Prato*

*Page 3.
coats of arms on the
Palazzo Vecchio
Florence*

*Pages 4–5.
Pine trees bordering a
vineyard near Monte
San Savino*

*Page 9.
a farm at sunset
Le Crete area*

EDITOR: *Susan Costello*
DESIGNER: *Patricia Fabricant*
TRANSLATOR: *John Goodman*
PRODUCTION EDITOR: *Abigail Asher*
PRODUCTION MANAGER: *Lou Bilka*
MAP: *Oliver Williams*

*First edition
2 4 6 8 10 9 7 5 3 1*

*ISBN 1-55859-895-2
LC Card Number: 95-34959*

Olive tree and irises
on hillside
Troghi

CONTENTS

PREFACE

by Sonja Bullaty & Angelo Lomeo

e have spent a good part of a year in Tuscany, spread over a span of 30 years. What we at first encountered in art is magically there, in reality—the trees and vineyards in a painting come to life on a Tuscan hillside.

The name means so much more than the region. It evokes the Renaissance, a place in time between the middle ages and modern times. The word Tuscany holds the secret to so many other names: Florence, Siena, Pisa; Botticelli, Giotto, Leonardo, Michelangelo, Raphael, Signorelli; Dante; the Medici; the Etruscans; early music; Chianti wines, and a way with food.

The strange thing is that so much of what we envisioned is still there, and the profusion is overwhelming—the art, the architecture, the landscape, the landscape in art and art in the landscape. Some of these landscapes go beyond the geographical confines of Tuscany, from the foothills of the Apennines in the Piedmont region, along the Ligurian sea, through the hilltowns of Tuscany and Umbria. They speak of a long tradition of love of the land.

A first visit to Tuscany can be daunting, even intimidating. There is so much to see, to experience, and to learn. There is too much of everything to absorb, including a multitude of museums, churches, duomos, towers, even labels of Chianti. But after a while the mind and the senses accept that no matter how many lifetimes are spent there, one cannot see it all. So we started to relax and enjoy and to look forward to new riches every day.

Like a kaleidoscope the landscape changes around each bend of the road. Each town has a distinct history and architecture, each village a different atmosphere and a different sensibility. Trying to do this justice in photographs is perhaps as exciting and challenging today as the study of chiaroscuro was to the artists of their day, who explored the play of light and shadow long before photography was born.

Since we first visited, some things have changed—people dress differently; cars intrude but make it possible to see more; Florence is overrun with tourists (but probably always was). There are crowds to see *David* by Michelangelo and to enter the Uffizi, but in the hills the olives take their time to ripen and so do the grapes, and here one can always find solitude. The old haystacks, true works of art, can still be found but are gradually giving way to more efficient methods of storing hay.

Some of our experiences will remain pictures only in our minds: the time the moon rose behind the orchestra in the courtyard of the Pitti Palace during a moving passage of music from the early Renaissance. The evening just after the sun had set in Vinci, Leonardo's birthplace, and we felt suspended in time, with the endless hills of olive trees dissolving into infinity and total silence. The uncanny feeling of being in the place in the Apuan Alps where Michelangelo so long ago chose his pieces of marble.

Then there was the time we got lost crossing the Apennines and almost wrecked our car, to be rewarded with a sea of *giaggiole* (irises), the symbol of Florence. Or a shared meal with friends, in their lovely Tuscan home, listening to the music of the Italian language and clinking glasses of wine grown on the hill above. And how does one capture the taste of freshly picked porcini cooked to perfection in the local olive oil?

In this part of Italy, "perspective" entered the vocabulary, and Tuscany still gives a special perspective on life. To us, one of the enduring legacies of Tuscany is the hope of becoming a Renaissance person. When the mind is challenged, and the senses are engaged, this development somehow seems possible.

THE LURE
OF TUSCANY

ERTAIN NAMES ARE FORMED from consonants and vowels whose exotic harmony sets us dreaming, for instance Samarkand, Madagascar, Kathmandu—and Patagonia, whose five syllables evoke a barren landscape populated only by sheep, rocks, and melancholy.

Close your eyes and pronounce the word "Tuscany." It summons up associations of earthly perfection, of images sprinkled with happiness, daubed with ocher and marble (white from Carrara, green from Prato, pink from the Maremma), and a cyprus-lined path that leads nowhere, an infinity of hills bathed in clear light blessed by the gods, a honey-colored villa glimpsed from a baroque garden, the perfume of olive oil, faded frescoes in silent cloisters—and a long procession of great men: Leonardo da Vinci, Machiavelli, Galileo, Michelangelo, Lorenzo de' Medici, Giotto, Petrarch, Dante, Pinocchio.

A Room with a View

OPEN YOUR EYES, take the train as far as Florence, and drink your first Italian coffee at the station there, which was built by Michelucci in 1935 and manages to be relatively inconspicuous in a landscape whose every street corner, whose every breeze, evokes centuries rich in historical incident. After having paid your 2,000 lire—don't panic, despite all those zeroes life here isn't expensive—the ideal thing would be to obtain a bird's-eye view of the city, taking in at a glance, in the morning mist, Arnolfo di Cambio's duomo, Brunelleschi's dome, Giotto's campanile, the Palazzo Vecchio and the Piazza della Signoria, the

Boboli Gardens (in which Henry James was delighted to find "neither parterres, nor pagodas, nor peacocks, nor swans"), the Ponte Vecchio and the Arno, of which Mark Twain wittily remarked: "It would be a very plausible river if they would pump some water into it. They call it a river, and they honestly think it is a river, do these dark and bloody Florentines. They even help out the delusion by building bridges over it. I do not see why they are too good to wade." He must have passed through the city in a period of drought, and Giono, too, for he says much the same thing, if in less ironical terms: "It is a river, of course, since it empties directly into the sea, but it's a river the way a cat is a tiger." However, two memorable floods came close to destroying Florence. In 1333 the Arno, having overflowed its banks, washed away bridges and devastated the city. And on November 4, 1966, a sea of mud engulfed shops, museums, and churches, notably in the Santa Croce quarter, sometimes reaching a depth of over thirteen feet (four meters), coating the great crucifix by Cimabue with a thick layer of oil and sweeping away thousands of books and manuscripts.

Today the city is impeccably clean, and no one walking its flagstone streets would let fall so much as a candy wrapper. As for Mark Twain's "dark and bloody Florentines," the phrase is a bit exaggerated. True, there were once some rather unpleasant scuffles between the Guelphs and the Ghibellines, between the Medici and the Pazzi clans, not to mention between Florence and Dante—who, having been banished from the city, relegated it to hell. But all that is now in the past. Visitors today will find that its inhabitants are exquisitely courteous.

"Florentines are the politest of men."
— STENDHAL

AFTER THIS COMPLIMENTARY OPENING, of course, Stendhal's portrait sours a bit, for in his view the members of this genus are also "the most exacting, the most faithful to their little calculations of expediency and economy. In the street, they all have the air of clerks . . . who, after having carefully brushed their suits themselves and waxed their boots, are hurrying to reach their offices at the appointed time." The Goncourt brothers were just as caustic, describing Florence as a city "where three-quarters of the streets smell bad, where the women wear doormats on their heads instead of hats, where the Arno, when there's any water in it, is the color of a café au lait." They also likened it to an English village "where the palaces are almost all a dreary black suggestive of London," while Alexandre Dumas, who spent a year there in 1839, observed that "at the end of autumn, a crowd of Englishmen of every rank, every sex, every age, and above all every color swarms into the

view from the Piazzale Michelangelo Florence

Tuscan capital." Dostoyevsky, who spent insomniac nights not far from the Palazzo Pitti, objected to the Florentine custom of singing through the night. And if we add that, in his *Voyage du Condottière*, André Suarès vilified with his customary enthusiasm "these soft and faded virgins, these numberless and empty-headed madonnas, these heaps of saints with their gesticulating fingers and uplifted arms, these boring, idiotic angels with their gaping mouths," it is tempting to conclude that famous travelers are often decidedly grouchy. (In fairness to Suarès, we should note that he saw so many marvels in the course of his five Italian trips that in the end he became demanding, all the more so since he was traveling on foot.) At the end of the nineteenth century, Emile Zola sensed something torpid about the city: "Former soldiers, actors having retired from the stage, all those of independent means with wooden beams and ropes, the *David* was dragged on rollers, upright, from the cathedral to the piazza by forty men, a task that consumed no less than four days (today it is a mere ten-minute walk for any tourist in reasonably good health). On the unveiling of this masterpiece, Michelangelo was acknowledged to be the greatest of all Italian sculptors; so this time the piece of marble had not been ruined. At least that's what most people will tell you. Myself, I find the young man's feet too short and his hands too large, and even if these flaws are the result of conscious calculation, the final result strikes me as labored and charmless. I would add that I find in the *Rondanini Pietà* and the *Deposition of Christ*—executed by the same Michelangelo at the end of his life and both generally considered unfinished—an intensity and an infinite sadness that, this time around, are the products of genius. But then—thank God!—no one is asking for my opinion.

"The traveler who has gone to Italy to study the tactile values of Giotto, or the corruption of the papacy, may return remembering nothing but the blue sky and the men and women who live under it."
— E. M. FORSTER

NOW, HAVING PAID FOR your coffee and realized that a bird's-eye view of the city is not a realistic possibility, walk toward Santa Maria Novella, which, very conveniently, is scarcely three hundred thirty feet (a hundred meters) from the train station. The gray-green marble volutes of its facade, the frescoes fading into evanescence in its green cloister (some of them by Uccello), the simple harmony of the inner gardens through which promenade, under the pure early morning sky, a few dreamers who are still half asleep, will instill in you a serene happiness that won't unduly increase your heart rate, a sense of well-being that has no need of psychiatric relief. Unlike Santa Croce, Santa Maria Novella is not depressing. And then it's situated on one of those curious Tuscan squares that seem to have been designed with languor and *far niente* specifically in view.

"It's there that Florence tried twenty times to be free."
— STENDHAL

IT IS INDEED THERE, in the Piazza della Signoria, which also has this daring, charming allure, although a bit cantankerous. The magnificent and severe Palazzo Vecchio seems to survey from on high the polyglot assemblage at its feet: a copy of the *David*, the original

Neptune splashing in its fountain, and the elegant Loggia dei Lanzi, in which Cellini's *Perseus* and a gaggle of Roman empresses, more ordinary women, and dying warriors carried by bearded men have been plunked down at random (so it seems, at least); the guidebooks say these works include an *Abduction of the Sabine Women* and an *Ajax Carrying the Body of Patroclus*.

This Piazza della Signoria has seen more than its share of drama. It was here that one of the members of the Pazzi conspiracy against the Medici was hanged—which rated him a place in the notebooks of Leonardo da Vinci, who, passing through the piazza while the body still was hanging from the noose, drew a sketch of it and jotted down the following annotation: "Little russet cap, black satin doublet, jerkin lined with black, blue mantle lined with black-and-white striped velvet. Bernardo de Bandino Baroncelli. Black stockings." These notes tell us a bit about contemporary dress but precious little about Leonardo's reaction to what he had just seen.

It was also here that Savonarola, a friar at the monastery of San Marco, the forecaster of apocalypse and divine lightning, was hanged and burned. But let's backtrack a bit: at the end of 1494, just as surely as Lorenzo de' Medici had governed Florence from the depths of his palace, Savonarola directed it from within his convent, even though he held no government post of any kind. Before long, this messianic puritan declared anything that even came close to qualifying as a sin to be anathema: games of chance, oaths, ribald songs, prostitution, horse racing, "indecent" female dress. Even the Maundy Thursday carnival before Easter, which had been celebrated in an atmosphere of almost pagan abandon, was turned into a stodgy religious festival. In 1497, Savonarola made an audacious move: he sent young men to shake down the city by demanding of each citizen that he turn over a "vanity," some symbol of the futility of earthly pleasure: jewelry, silk, playing cards, licentious books, etc. The booty continued to pile up in the piazza until the last night of carnival, when, to the accompaniment of church bells, the bonfire was lit. After playing along with their "redeemer" for a while, the Florentines, who are known to be fickle in their affections, lost patience with his excesses and resolved to rid themselves of him. Savonarola, whose zealotry was feeding on itself, attacked Pope Alexander VI (who was not, it's true, a model of virtue), was excommunicated, responded by "excommunicating" the pope in turn, and, one thing having led to another, found himself imprisoned in the palazzo with two of his aides and submitted to all manner of torture. Finally, on May 23, 1498, all three were hanged and burned on the very spot where they had raised their bonfire of the vanities, and their ashes were scattered in the Arno—a satisfying conclusion to the story, for it fulfilled Savonarola's own prophecy that the wicked "would seize hold of the just and burn them in the center of the city; and that which the fire does not consume and the wind does not blow away will be thrown by them into the river."

"'Savonarola's martyrdom here in Florence,' wrote Mrs. Browning,
'is scarcely worse than Flush's in the summer.'"
— VIRGINIA WOOLF

PERHAPS MRS. BROWNING exaggerates a bit. The martyrdom suffered by the dog Flush was fleas, which invade Florentine houses every summer. In fact, in the middle of the nineteenth century all Italy was renowned for its fleas; in the words of Nathaniel Hawthorne, "We were speaking of fleas—those insects that, in Rome, enter into everyone's most intimate concerns."

But what's the connection between the poet Elizabeth Barrett Browning, Florence, Flush, and Virginia Woolf?

A brief flashback: Once upon a time there was Elizabeth Barrett who, smothered by a tyrannical father, led the existence of an invalid, spending her days reclining amid cushions and books. In 1842, an old lady gave her a young cocker spaniel named Flush, who was happy to spend his days at the feet of his mistress's sofa until the arrival on the scene of a certain Robert Browning, poet by profession. Abruptly, at age forty, Elizabeth was revitalized, married Robert Browning in secret, and fled with him—and Flush—to Italy. There, the magic of the Tuscan hills completed the miracle—with the help of a little Chianti: "Now, for instance, instead of sipping a thimbleful of port and complaining of the headache, she tossed off a tumbler of chianti and slept the sounder." This mad love was to last sixteen years, until Elizabeth's death.

In 1933, Virginia Woolf had the wonderful idea of recounting this mythic love story through the life and feelings of Flush, an arrangement that, among its many advantages, gave her an excuse to write about Tuscany from a dog's point of view. Rather snobbish about his aristocratic breeding, which had the imprimatur of the Kennel Club, Flush discovered to his stupefaction that he was "the only pure-born cocker spaniel in the whole of Pisa." The couple subsequently settled in Florence and Flush began to keep low company. "He was becoming daily more and more democratic." In fact, he led the life of a knockabout, having free run of all the city's streets. Virginia Woolf did not waste this choice opportunity to evoke Florentine life as filtered through a canine infatuation—a little spaniel with whom he spent the night, while the torch-bearing populace marched through the streets chanting "Viva Leopoldo Secondo"—and, of course, his sense of smell: "He followed the swooning sweetness of incense into the violet intricacies of dark cathedrals; and, sniffing, tried to lap the gold on the window-stained tomb." Flush licked the toes of statues, tasted and disgorged macaroni, went to sleep in a pool of sunlight, crossed every threshold, tested the sweetness of every marble, and absorbed the city's past in his own way: "Upon the infinitely sensitive pads of his feet he took the clear stamp of proud Latin inscriptions." And then one day, having grown old, he began to prefer shadow to sunlight and started to recount his long story to younger Florentine dogs. "The peasants in the market arranged beds of leaves for him under their large baskets, and even threw him bunches of grapes from time to time. He was known and loved by all Florence—nobles and rustics, dogs and men."

"Farewell Florence, the most beautiful museum of all."
— *ANDRÉ SUARÈS*

IF YOU'RE AT ALL SENSITIVE, then you'd do well to steer clear of the Stendhal syndrome by leaving Florence and its torment of fleas. Depart for the south, where an entire population of Etruscan ghosts sleeps by the side of the road. Head for the broad flatlands of Maremma, once a swamp infested with malaria. Or for the marble quarries of Carrione, close to Cararra, which resemble glaciers. There you'll see *statuario,* the pure white marble preferred by Michelangelo, as well as other varieties—striated with gray and vaguely turquoise, yellow with black veins, orange-tinted—charmingly called *Fior di pesco, Breccia violetta,* and *Arabescato.* Descend into the forests of Monte Argentario and the pine-lands of

springtime near Volterra

Orbetello, in Porto Santo Stefano, and, from there, proceed to the little island of Giglio, a paradise of pines, fig trees, and oaks with magnificent beaches lining marvelous inlets. Follow the tortuous roadways of Pitigliano, at the summit of ocher cliffs from which pieces sometimes tumble. Or head north, into the sweet flowered valleys of the Garfagnana, where you can see a strange crooked bridge supposedly built by the devil. If you should be seized by a strong desire to see something that looks like it came out of a painting by Giotto, go to his native Mugello. John Ruskin visited there in the nineteenth century: "There are neither gardens nor flowers nor dazzling palace walls, only a gray stretch of mountainous ground with occasional stands of green oaks and olive trees." Save for the addition of a few telephone poles, the Mugello valley still has this wild, solitary character.

Left.
olive tree
southern Tuscany

Right.
shrine in a hilltown
Todi

Of course wherever you go you'll find frescoes, Etruscan tombs, wall escutcheons, churches, and other traces of the past—but incognito, without trumpets or the aura of fame, a past that floats in the air like a perfume, sweetening and seasoning everything around you. And on the roads you'll pass quite a few free-wheeling Vespas with their helmeted drivers; the very sight of them will lighten your mood.

There exist in Tuscany a good number of wonderful little places never mentioned in most guidebooks because no Medici ever set foot there and there's no masterpiece to act as a draw. We won't even speak, for instance, of Chiara in Prumiano, "a splendid seventeenth-century villa, the heart of a little medieval town." The place has no history to speak of; it's lost in the vineyards, its inhabitants eat off of wine casks—it's in the middle of nowhere and you'd never find it. On the other hand, you might manage to find Barberino Val d'Elsa, a fortified village perched in Chianti, where life is good because the deeply shadowed facades, which seem so formidable, have a secret: the backs of these buildings open onto a view of hills extending to the horizon, to Livorno, whose lighthouse is visible on clear nights, which is to say when there aren't too many stars, nor too many clouds—rarely, in sum, but one knows that it exists, and the sea, too, at the end of the prospect.

In the Shadow of the Lighthouse, a Few Legendary Silhouettes

IT WAS FROM LIVORNO THAT, one day in the summer of 1822, Percy Shelley and his friend Williams set sail—leaving Mary Shelley, the author of *Frankenstein*, at home—and were carried off by a storm. The sea surrendered their bodies two weeks later. Before meeting this watery end, Shelley had been living on the coast, where he wrote his tragedy *The Cenci* and, inspired by another storm over the bay of Lerici, his *To a Skylark*. He had also lived in Pisa, in a palace close to the house in which Galileo was born, not far from his friend Byron, who, on that awful day, built a funeral pyre on the beach near Viareggio. He maintained that, after the body had been consumed by the flames, Shelley's heart remained intact—but then Shelly and Byron were romantics.

It was also in Livorno, in 1884, that Amedeo Modigliani was born. A romantic legend was woven around him, too, by his family, friends, and a host of others since, obscuring the real man in a hackneyed fantasy about a painter whose existence was cursed. For example, according to this legend, at age fourteen, when he had yet to manifest the slightest artistic inclination, young Amedeo fell into a delirium induced by typhoid fever, which somehow prompted his passion for images. It would also have us believe that he struggled against inept parents who wanted him to pursue a career in business. In reality, two years before his typhoid he was already pestering his mother about drawing lessons, and this same mother certainly had not envisioned him as a businessman, for she noted in her journal how ravished she was at seeing her "Dedo" abandon his studies and plunge enthusiastically into painting. She found that he "doesn't paint too badly and draws quite well." Clearly she was proud of him. As for the dates of the various sojourns in Livorno, these vary according to the importance attributed by Modigliani's various biographers to his Italian patriotism. In any case, in 1898 he frequented the post-Macchiaioli studio of Micheli and spent his Sundays painting in the countryside around Livorno. The journalist Gastone Razzaguta, who set out to make him appear an authentic Tuscan ruined by Paris, described him as follows: "When Amedeo Modigliano, known as Dedo, was a distinguished, disciplined, and studious young man in the studio of Micheli, he drew carefully and without the least bit of distortion." He described his way of "almost always representing his subjects with their hands on their knees" as typically Tuscan, and concluded: "In the end, what's in question is a peaceable indigenous vision that emigrated and took on a dramatic cast in France." Others maintain that the painter's Italian origins are of negligible importance; they think his genius flowered in the Parisian atmosphere of drunkenness, debauchery, and misery. Doubtless the real Modigliani is somewhere between these two extremes, but it's difficult to pin him down.

We do know, however, that in 1902 he enrolled in the Free School of the Nude in Florence and, the following year, in the Free School of the Nude in Venice, where he cut classes to sketch in cafes and in bordellos. Gastone Razzaguta describes him, bursting into the Café Bardi, as pale, aggressive, with shaven head, his pants held up by a bit of rope and espadrilles on his feet. "He says that he returned to Livorno because he loves these comfortable, economical shoes and cecinata." During this last summer in Livorno he no longer talked about painting. He was determined to become a sculptor and persisted in showing photos of his carved pieces to friends in hopes of winning their admiration, but they responded to these "elongated heads with long straight noses" only with skepticism and indifference. However, they found a shed near the market for him and he set to work on a number of stone blocks—the ones then used to pave streets. But no one saw the results. "When he decided to return to Paris, he asked us where he could store his sculptures, which were all in this shed. Did they really exist? Who knows? Perhaps Modigliani took them with him, or perhaps he took our friendly advice. We all gave him the same answer: throw them into the canal." (Many years later, the canal was dredged and three carved heads were recovered and duly authenticated; they had already been earmarked for exhibition in the Livorno Museum when three students confessed they were fakes.) After this sad episode in Livorno, Modigliani wrote his mother, in winter 1919, that he hoped to return in the spring, but he died on January 24, 1920, of tuberculosis—and not, as legend has it, of hunger, alcohol, and despair. But this legend now took off like a rocket: supposedly, in his last moments he invited Jeanne Hébutern to follow him "so he could have his favorite model in paradise," avowed to Ortis de Zarate that only "a little

*young grapevines
near Val d'Elsa*

piece of brain" was still functioning, and, while being transported to the hospital, was overcome with longing for his lost homeland and murmured "Cara Italia"—all of which, in the view of Jeanne Modigliani, makes "rather too many last words for any single man."

In any case, after the bombing of the Second World War all that remained of old Livorno—with its magnificent avenues lined with villas and palazzi, and its canals, along which the young Amedeo strolled—were a few ramshackle palazzi, some warehouses, and a scattering of fish markets.

> *"Very little difference between the color of the sky and that of olive trees: it's a bluish wash; in the leaves there's a bit more cinders. Nowhere does one see the raw azure that prompts the beatific admiration of hot-blooded temperaments."*
> — *JEAN GIONO*

DURING THE DAY, from the terrace of Barberigo, there's no chance of seeing the Livorno lighthouse. Shelley and Modigliani are forgotten, one is transported by the "bluish wash" that sometimes tends toward mauve, or gold, or pure transparency. Unlike Normandy, which plays to perfection its role as a greenish platform for bovines, the Tuscan countryside, like the sea, like the desert, puts you in an apt frame of mind for contemplating the sky, and eternity. Happiness is a tangible presence here. It rides the wind, seeming to have come from very far away, and permeates the ceaselessly changing light that gives the soil its special soul. This happiness penetrates so deeply that it seems like a kind of laziness: you're seized by a desire to remain still, to do nothing, or *far niente,* as the Italians say, rather than playing the tourist and making rushed visits to all the places listed in the guide-books that close at 4 P.M. sharp.

However, in Tuscany certain visits are obligatory. It wouldn't be decent to return from there and tell your friends: No, I didn't see San Marco and the frescoes by Fra Angelico, nor the Giottos in Santa Croce, nor the Masaccios in the Carmine, nor any Raphaels, nor the three sets of bronze Baptistry doors (the most famous of which, executed by Ghiberti, are known as the "Gates of Paradise" because Michelangelo judged them to be worthy of leading to that sacred precinct), nor the portrait of Dante by Giotto in the Bargello chapel, nor all the Virgin-and-Childs, Trinities, Annunciations, Madonnas, Adorations, and Crucifixions—not to mention the occasional battle scene—to be found in even the least important churches and the most obscure chapels.

As for the terrible question, "And the Uffizi?", referring to the celebrated museum with more than a million visitors annually and close to four thousand works, about 1,800 of which are visible only by special appointment, you have to answer "No," for you decided to not even attempt to get in, realizing it would be pointless to view Botticelli's *Primavera* through a dense crowd uttering banalities in all known languages. Instead of waiting your turn in a line more than eight hundred yards long, you took the several steps necessary to reach the Arno and remained there, leaning over a parapet, with an impregnable view of a pigeon, itself lost in contemplation of the Ponte Vecchio. You cannot avow such offhandedness—or phlegm, or lack of resolve. Especially since Tuscany is not conducive to indifference, being full of passionate beings, both presently and in its historical annals. Mention Scotland and everybody says it rains a lot and leaves the matter there. But when it comes to Tuscany, you're expected to state your views about Florentine palazzi (Are they beautiful or not?), to declare that, in the end, Pontormo is not as great as Rosso (or the reverse), to opine that such and such a painting is surely by Leonardo (or is not by him), to maintain that Botticelli is superior to Rembrandt and Dürer (or the reverse), to return Ghirlandaio to his rightful place (allowing him a charming vivacity at best, in much the way those who admire Beethoven dismiss Mozart), and to discern in Michelangelo a Dantean failure of taste—like Suarès, who detested the Medici tombs, finding the reclining figures of Night and Day to be not women but "athletes with breasts." To sum up, in this febrile atmosphere in which everybody's set afire by something, you're fully aware that

irises and grapevines
Poggio alla Croce

everything's worth visiting, but, deliciously ensconced in your recliner on the terrace in Barberino, you can barely summon enough energy to lift your nose and sniff out the direction of the wind.

The fact that this laziness will be cause for regret one day only makes it that much sweeter. And in fact, on the eve of your departure you realize that spending a whole day wandering aimlessly instead of making the trip to Siena was a huge mistake.

"Before crossing the threshold of Siena, whether from the north or from the south, one approaches through a lunar valley."
— *ANDRÉ SUARÈS*

"We advance slowly, through a set of small volcanic hills covered with grapevines and small olive trees: nothing uglier."
— STENDHAL

"NOTHING UGLIER," proclaimed Stendhal, who had already made known his view that Florence was situated "in the middle of threadbare mountains." Decidedly, he should have just stayed home. But by now you know that you would have loved these chalky hills, these valleys without trees and without villages, and all the aridity that, in the area around Siena, reverts to real countryside and, with its fig trees, olive trees, grapevines, and heavy peach perfume, almost resembles a kitchen garden.

Now you know just how much you'd have loved this red city, simpler and warmer than Florence, less weighed down by history, a city in lights and darks enriched by balconies, nooks, alleyways, and dead-end streets. You'd have loved the Campo, the open square paved with a brick that hesitates between red, pink, and ocher, and that, depending on whom you talk to, is shaped like a tilted shell, a holy-water stoop, a fan, or an immense sundial on which the shadow of the Torre del Mangia, inching across the surface, tells you the morning's over, that the sun is at its height, that it's descending, that it's disappearing and the hour

Piazza del Campo
Siena

is nigh for drinking a glass of vin santo. You know because people have told you: it's hard to explain, but this square is the spot on earth where one feels happiest.

In summer you can sit on the ground and have a conversation, except for July 2 and August 16, the days set aside for the famous Palio. You know, the horse race that lasts a minute and ten seconds but has been in preparation since the previous year—for centuries, in fact. Even after being prettified for tourists, the Palio remains archaic and violent. The jockeys ride bareback, anything goes (including tricks and bribery), and every *contrada*, or quarter, sets out to smash the others. The day before, all the city's *contrade* mount celebrations, and on the morning of the event all the horses are blessed in their local church. It's still surprising to see a horse in a church, its magnificent body so out of place, puzzled by the sumptuousness of this curious stable. The race begins in an atmosphere of total hysteria, and, three circuits and a cloud of dust later, one of the *contrade* has won the *palio*, or "rag": a hand-painted silk banner. This time the victorious horse is honored in the cathedral, in the adoring presence of all Siena. What does the animal think of this Santa Maria dell'Assunta (to give its full name), chock full of black marble, and white marble, and statues of popes and emperors, which reminds some of a bizarre pastry but for others—including Wagner—is pure splendor? What does the horse make of it? We'll never know. What matters is that he's won. And if his rider fell off along the way, no matter. He's the hero of the day, and his great fame will have the place of honor at the victory banquet, when at midnight the Torre del Mangia casts a long lunar shadow over the Piazza del Campo.

"And flung into the depths of the sky, looking for the moon, the tallest and most ravishing of the towers rises in a single bound, so robust yet so delicate, so strong yet so light that it's like a pink lily that's pushed its way through the snow."
— ANDRÉ SUARÈS

TORRE DEL MANGIA is the tallest of the towers because things were decided so. Built between 1325 and 1348, it was intended to surpass everything then extant in Italy, especially the tower of the Palazzo Vecchio in Florence, its rival. The Torre del Mangia indeed won the palm, rising 337 feet (102 meters) as opposed to the 310 feet (94 meters) of the Florentine structure. But twenty-seven feet (eight meters) of stone is a fragile symbol of superiority. And after more than a century of combat, after a few victories and as many defeats, after the great plague of 1348 (which claimed thousands, Petrarch's sweet Laura among them), Siena, under siege by Florentine and German forces in 1555, understood that this defeat would be the last and resorted to desperate measures in hopes of avoiding it: food being scarce, useless mouths were put to death, beginning with abandoned children. All for nought: Siena fell to Florence, as had Arezzo and Pisa before it. One can still encounter elderly Sienese who take the whole episode personally, as though they themselves had been forced to participate in this horror by murdering their children.

The Torre was not alone in its will to victory. In those days, towers rose into the sky like so many emblems of power and arrogance. In 1334, when Florence placed Giotto in charge of construction at the cathedral, the contract stipulated "that the campanile be so constructed as to surpass in magnificence, height, and quality everything of the kind built by the Greeks and Romans at the height of their grandeur" and, specifically, that it surpass the tower in Pisa, which, still incomplete and beginning to lean (it began to tip soon

field of mustard and grapevines near San Gimignano

THE LURE OF TUSCANY

after construction began in 1174), promised to be a marvel of grace and beauty. That tower wasn't *meant* to lean, of course. But it would seem that erroneous information on this point began to circulate, for in the seventeenth century the writer John Evelyn praised the structure as follows: "Anyone looking at it expects to see it fall over, so successful has the architect been in making it lean with astonishing skill; the fact that it still stands must leave more than one mathematician amazed." To be sure—all the more so as this little flaw has worsened over time, to the delight of tourists and the growing concern of Pisa's inhabitants.

The fact remains that, before dying, Giotto saw the lower levels of his own campanile rise, and the structure is such a miracle of grace and strength that Charles V, whose army wrought devastation the entire length and breadth of Italy but who was a man of taste, described it as a "precious jewel that should be kept under a glass cover."

But the most hallucinatory vestige of this obsession with verticality is San Gimignano, such as Henry James saw it, "with its mutilated marks of adjustment to the extinct type of creature it once harboured figuring against the sky as maimed gesticulating arms flourished in protest against its fate." In an earlier era, San Gimignano "delle belle Torri" boasted at least seventy towers. Only thirteen have survived (or fourteen: accounts vary), but these still give it a fantastic, unreal quality when seen from far away, set amid hills covered with grapevines, olive trees, and cypresses. The first tower was called "la Rognosa," and construction of any higher ones was expressly forbidden. But San Gimignano, which had been at war for fifteen years—with Volterra, Pistoia, Colle, Arezzo, Florence, and the entire earth—was also wracked by internal disputes between a Guelph family (the Ardinghellis) and a Ghibelline one (the Salvuccis). Each clan endeavored to raise its towers higher than those of its neighbors, higher than "la Rognosa," until Florence settled matters by taking control of the city in 1353.

All that remains of these virile clashes and guttings is a marvelous medieval town awash in soft hues that absolutely must be visited in early morning or late afternoon; otherwise, you'll find yourself engulfed in a sea of humanity.

Everything in San Gimignano is as it should be: the narrow streets, the marriage of stone and brick, the gray towers, the ocher towers, the flowers, the hazelnut gelato, the frescoes, the Piazza della Cisterna. Every corner has its point of beauty. For example, your feet hurt, you sit down in the arcade of the little Piazza Pecori long enough to smoke a cigarette—despite it's not being good for you—while you admire the sunlight playing over the ten different shades of ocher on the wall across the way. You have occasion to turn around, and suddenly you're cheek-by-jowl with a little Annunciation by Ghirlandaio tucked away in the shadows, as discreet as can be, asking only to pass unnoticed, its beauty providing delight enough for a whole lifetime.

*"Suddenly we heard a cock crow pierce the air in an
almost supernatural way. Count Dracula, leaping up, cried:
"What! Morning already, yet again!""*

ASIDE FROM TOWERS, Tuscany has two specialties: *bruschetta*—toasted bread rubbed with garlic and dipped in olive oil, eaten as a snack with a glass of vin santo—and bats, whose nocturnal silhouettes harmonize perfectly, both aesthetically and emotionally, with nights of the full moon. Alexandre Vialatte, whose curiosity led him to study a number of odd subjects—the sadness of the hippopotamus, for example, and the uncontrollable proliferation of hyacinth in the rivers of Africa—became fascinated with this mythic creature. According to him, scientists long perceived a resemblance between bats and men (thanks to their pectoral teats, some authors even made unflattering comparisons with Madame de Pompadour), to such an extent that Carl von Linnaeus, the famous Swedish naturalist of the eighteenth century, classed them, along with monkeys, as primates. It was only after the invention of the microscope that this theory was abandoned. But Vialatte—who had common sense to spare—thought that most scientists could drown in a glass of water, and that sometimes it is best to remain ignorant. He pointed out that no one ever confused them in practice, and that "it was never proposed to send bats to war, and it was always men who were obliged to pay taxes."

These charming creatures fly through the Tuscan night making velvety noises and tracing arcs redolent of dreams. "Fly" is not really the right word, though, for bats, like dolphins, move about by means of ultrasound waves, which, once emitted, redound in the form of echoes that allow them to get their bearings. As a result they seem to glide without rhyme or reason when, the last rays of the sun having been swallowed up by the distant hills, they emerge from their lairs to commence their fantastic nocturnal wanderings. You're drinking a glass of vin santo and munching on *bruschetta,* and these little animals—which are neither birds nor mice, and certainly not mosquitoes!—observe you with their wrinkled faces. It's quite moving, in the end. Several times I've been awake at five-fifteen—in the morning!—and so have been privileged to witness their ritual of return. For that is the precise hour when, in July, the night begins to give out, when colors have not yet edged into visibility and everything is bathed in an unreal gray. It's then that the bats, half-vampires, half-Cinderellas, beat a hasty retreat to their sanctuaries under pain of seeing their coaches turn into pumpkins or, more serious, of themselves crumbling into dust. They pass before your window, the rush of air in their wake brushes against your skin (which revives infantile fears, for every child knows that bats like to get their little claws into your hair), they disappear into a hole and then come out again as if savoring the possibilities. "Do I still have time to amuse myself with this frightened animal at the window, or do I really have to call it a night?" Some of the more audacious ones continue circling about, but most defer to the imperious sun and disappear at dawn's first glow.

"Leonardo da Vinci bores me. He should have kept to his flying machines."
— AUGUSTE RENOIR

WE MIGHT WELL WONDER whether Leonardo didn't tell himself the same thing when, at about age fifty, he started working on his famous ornithopter (which was never to fly), himself studying bats, observing their silky flight and dissecting their wings in hopes of understanding their magic. Previously, in 1482, discouraged by the indifference of the Medici toward him, he had sought the protection of Duke Sforza by writing him an extremely curious letter in which he presented himself as an expert on things military, mentioning "very light and very resistant" bridges, designs for cannon that would be "very convenient and easy to transport," and all manner of catapults "and other machines of marvelous efficiency." At the end of this enticing catalog, he added two sentences stating that he was also a painter and a sculptor.

In any case, he produced only a dozen paintings in the course of his sixty-seven years; his celebrated notebooks contain more than seven thousand pages of text and drawings. His entries about his own life are just as dry as his description of the hanged man in the Piazza della Signoria. The day his father died, he wrote: "On July 9, 1504, Wednesday at seven o'clock, died Ser Piero da Vinci, my father, a notary in the Palazzo del Podestà, at seven o'clock. He was eighty years old, left ten sons and two daughters." Was it due to emotion or to distraction that he twice specified the time and increased his father's age by three years? No one can say. If we add that he wrote from right to left and that his manuscripts must be read with the aid of a mirror, the mystery quotient increases.

Conversely, his notebooks are full of very clear drawings of propellers, cranes, and mechanical shovels, a parachute, a windmill, a life-buoy, a proto-tank shaped like a flying saucer, and an "aerial" map of Tuscany—truly astounding, given that the ornithopter never flew and the map cannot really have been taken from the air. And also depictions of floods, volcanic eruptions, the human anatomy (a drawing of a fetus in the womb), and musical instruments of his own invention, including a rolling tamborine that beats time to the rhythm of its turning wheels. For Leonardo was the jack-of-all-trades as genius, a mind of truly extraordinary brilliance. But he had acquired an unfortunate reputation for abandoning projects he'd started before completing them—which may explain the Medici's resolve to ignore him.

Whereas Michelangelo was taken up by Lorenzo the Magnificent after having worked in Ghirlandaio's *bottega* for only a year. According to the historian Condivi, "Lorenzo, having come and observed the child's goodness and simplicity, envisioned great things for him. . . . As protector of all talents, he resolved to aid and assist such a spirit by taking him into his household." Michelangelo was barely fifteen when he went to live in the Medici palace. He lived side by side with the Medici children and his education was overseen by the paternal eye of Lorenzo; he read Dante and Petrarch and perfected his skills with the chisel (he always preferred to work in marble and detested bronze). As Condivi put it, "Michelangelo was coddled and encouraged in his honorable work," and this agreeable existence continued for three years, until Lorenzo's death on April 8, 1492.

"It is I who will remain and he who will leave."
— SAVONAROLA

SAVONAROLA HAD PREDICTED Lorenzo's premature end. "Even though I am from another city while he is from this one, and is even the first citizen of this city, it is I who will remain and he who will leave: I will remain, not he." But he had not imagined the terrible events that, so it is claimed, announced the death of "il Magnifico." According to legend, while he was in his death throes at his childhood residence in Careggi, lightning struck the dome of the Duomo, a comet flashed through the sky, wolves howled, the lions in the zoo killed one another, and, as dawn broke, the body of one of his doctors was discovered at the bottom of a well. A suicide? Murdered? In any case, Lorenzo was only forty-three years old and had been suffering from an attack of gout, a touch of rheumatic fever, and a stomach infection—in short, nothing life-threatening. But his doctors did him in by feeding him a mixture of pearls and precious stones thought to cure all ills.

"'When death weeps, it's a sign the healing has begun,' the raven said solemnly.
'I regret to contradict my illustrious colleague and friend,' said the screech-owl,
'but, as I see it, when death weeps it's a sign he doesn't want to die.'"
— CARLO COLLODI

THIS EDIFYING MEDICAL EXCHANGE occurred at the bedside of Pinocchio, at the house of the blue-haired fairy, and if he weeps, it's simply because he's alive. And one understands immediately that, contrary to widespread belief, Pinocchio was not born in the Walt

Disney studio but rather in a period when, despite the considerable advances in medical science since Lorenzo's day, it was still relatively dangerous to fall sick.

The puppet with the nose-that-grows-when-he-lies was brought into the world in Florence, in 1881, by the writer Carlo Lorenzini, who, after attaining his majority, took the name Carlo Collodi. (If you ever find yourself in the vicinity of the town of Collodi, be sure to visit the wonderful gardens of the Villa Garzoni, where fountains and trained vegetation combine with balustrades, stairways, and statues to produce extraordinary pictures in ocher and red.) Tuscany then being under the control of Austria, the young Collodi, who had developed a taste for freedom in the Piatti library, where he worked during the day, and at the Caffè Elvetichino, where he spent his evenings, began in 1848 to support the war of independence, published his first political articles in the *Lampion,* and commented on Florence's being named the capital of Italy in 1865 as follows: "And thus Florence remarries, taking as her spouse a vagabond who has wandered all over Italy identifying himself only with the transparent incognito 'Italian government.'" Five years later, Florence emerged from this union weakened and bruised. Collodi, who wrote for the newspaper *Fanfulla* and was becoming quite annoyed with the leaders implementing unification, reached a new level of sarcasm with his article "Delenda Toscana," in which he caustically suggested to Minister Minghetti that he simply remove Tuscany from the map of the nation and divide it into farms and subsidiary lease plots rather than prefectures and sub-prefectures. A dark and bitter thing, Collodi's sense of humor was well suited to the harsh times. And poor Tuscany, where soon the old furniture-maker Gepetto was to carve from a recalcitrant piece of wood a marionette to be christened Pinocchio: "This name will bring him luck. I knew a whole family of Pinocchi, and they all lived well. The richest among them was a beggar."

When Collodi sent the beginning of his story to the *Corriere dei Piccoli,* the leading Italian children's magazine, apparently he didn't put much stock in it. He called it a "childish thing" and asked only that he be paid enough to give him the courage to continue. He got as far as chapter XV—the terrible moment in which Pinocchio, hanged from a large oak tree, is on the verge of surrendering to solitude and despair—and then stopped work, maintaining that the story should end with the following words: "When, after he had waited and waited and still no one came, he thought about his poor father and, almost in agony, cried out: 'Oh! My papa, my papa! If only you were here!' But he lacked the breath to continue. He closed his eyes, opened his mouth, relaxed his legs, and, after a violent jolt, remained still, as though paralyzed."

A flabbergasting close, truly calculated to delight the *bambini!* However, in the weeks following the doll's hanging, the *Corriere* received neither complaints nor expressions of sorrow and concern from its young readers. Nobody cared one way or the other—except the editor, who protested and succeeded in having Pinocchio resurrected. Result? The puppet's adventures have been translated into just about every known language (including Latin and Esperanto), he was taken up by the Disney studio, and he has been subjected to structuralist analyses in which poor devils wrack their brains dissecting the "leximatics" of Collodi's text. This fortunate intervention also led to Fellini's adopting Pinocchio as one of his spiritual godfathers: the first time he went to the circus, sitting on his father's knee amid all the lights, applause, and drums, he had the impression the clowns were waiting for him and recognized him, "just like the puppets in Mangiafuoco when they saw Pinocchio on the stage and greeted him as one of their own, calling him by name, embracing him and dancing with him through the night."

In the years 1937–38, Fellini, fresh out of high school, got his start in Florence in the offices of the publisher Nerbini, which then produced several cartoon publications on a daily basis as well as the humorous weekly *420* (named after the gauge of Big Bertha, a 420-mm howitzer, the cannon that bombarded Paris). On the staff of *420,* the young Fellini, who knew perfectly well what he did not want to be—a lawyer, an engineer, or an admiral—but was still unsure of his vocation (though he was tempted to become a comic actor), was "something between the receptionist and an associate editor." In short, he put stamps on envelopes. Then, the importation of American comic strips like "Flash Gordon" being precluded by political tensions between Italy and the United States, he bravely commenced fabricating stories while Toppi, the principal draftsman at Nerbini, did his best to imitate Alex Raymond's drawing style. Such were the modest beginnings of the great Fellini, now renowned throughout the world.

"La pazzia bestialissima" (The Most Beastly Madness)

LET'S RETURN TO LEONARDO and his little problem: never being able to finish anything. Take the *Battle of Anghiari,* for instance. Around 1503, the Florentine government resolved to decorate the Great Hall of the Palazzo della Signoria with immense painted murals depicting heroic episodes in the city's history. Machiavelli, exploiting his status as secretary to the Florentine republic, obtained for Leonardo the greatest commission of his career: the *Battle of Anghiari*—in point of fact, a mere scuffle in which only one man died but that clinched the Florentine victory over the Milanese in 1440. Leonardo had just returned from having served Cesare Borgia in his recent military campaigns, during which he drew maps while his new friend Machiavelli took notes for *The Prince.* Leonardo was determined to get into his *Battle* his feelings about war: that it was *la pazzia bestialissima.*

*olive trees in
Leonardo's birthplace
Vinci*

Michelangelo, whose *David* was still in its shed awaiting transport to the Piazza della Signoria, was also involved in the project and was preparing a *Battle of Cascina* for the other end of the same wall. Leonardo was fifty, whereas Michelangelo was twenty-eight. There is no evidence that the Signoria, in choosing them, was consciously pitting them against one another. But in fact, Michelangelo did his best to surpass Leonardo, whom he had always disliked. Leonardo struck him as a courtier and an opportunist. And then his beauty, his powers of seduction, his enormous self-confidence, his infinite array of talents—he even sang and improvised superbly on the lyre—were destined to irritate the tormented and timid Michelangelo, who wrote in one of his sonnets: "As for me, my happiness is melancholy."

In the end, this battle of titans fell rather flat, for neither Leonardo nor Michelangelo managed to bring their fresco to completion. They did finish their cartoons, or worked-up compositional drawings on paper, and artists from all over Italy came to Florence to study them. The young Raphael was among the admirers of these drawings, as was Benvenuto Cellini, although a mere six years old at the time. Leonardo attacked the fresco itself in the spring of 1504. He profited from the occasion to try out new materials and a tempera technique that, according to him, would fix the image more securely to the surface. But the results were catastrophic: the colors faded and the paint ran.

Leonardo was fond of experimenting: he had previously encountered similar problems with his *Last Supper,* on the wall of the refectory in the Dominican convent of Santa Maria delle Grazie, in Milan. There he covered the perpetually damp wall with a protective coating of his own devising—a mixture of pitch and mastic—that proved noxious. When Vasari saw the fresco in 1556, by which time it had also been damaged by a flood, this supreme masterpiece was a "muddle of blots." Over the centuries the *Last Supper* has been the object of numerous restoration campaigns, some of them disastrous (hence the famous "Ode on the Death of a Masterpiece" by Gabriele d'Annunzio), but in 1946 the master technician Mauro Pellicioli went to work on it, and eight years later it had been restored as close as it will ever be to Leonardo's original vision.

In short, discouraged by the runs in his *Battle of Anghiari* (which survives in the form of copies by his biographer Vasari, and Rubens), Leonardo stopped working on it, much to the irritation of the Signoria, which was anxious to minimize unnecessary expenditures. But, even if circumstances had been more auspicious, would he have brought the project to completion? This seems doubtful, for the *Battle* had ceased to interest him. He quickly moved on to his next project, the portrait of a twenty-four-year-old Florentine woman known as Monna Lisa (a shortened version of Madonna Lisa), the third wife of the merchant Francesco di Bartolommeo del Giocondo. This was the picture he managed to complete, and—God only knows why—it has become the most famous and most copied portrait in the world. There are more or less viable repetitions of the *Mona Lisa* all over the globe: the one in the Vernon collection, in the United States (which its owners insist is authentic), has an adolescent pout; the one in the Chamber of Deputies in Rome, attributed to one of Leonardo's students, is very puffy; that in the Walters Art Gallery in Baltimore is struggling to stay awake. As for those in the Oslo museum, in the Prado, in the collection of Dr. Carl Muller of Switzerland (an especially dreadful one), in the collection of Lord Spencer in Northampton, and in the Accademia Carrara in Bergamo (these last two are represented nude), they are so far from the original that there can be no doubt about their status as copies. And then there are the many versions that have never pretended to be the real thing, including many sculpted paraphrases and the naughty recension concocted by Marcel Duchamp, with its famous beard and mustache.

*"I am bruised, exhausted, worn out: such is the fruit of my efforts;
death is the inn where, having paid my dues, I'll have bed and board."*
— MICHELANGELO

AS FOR MICHELANGELO, he never even started to paint his *Battle of Cascina*, for he was summoned to Rome by Julius II, the "warrior pope," with whom he was to have stormy relations for several years. Julius loved the battlefield, but, on returning to the Vatican after having massacred the enemies of God, he cultivated the arts, with a little help from his stable of architects, painters, and sculptors selected by him to realize his ambitious schemes. He commissioned Michelangelo, among other things, to create frescoes on the Sistine Chapel ceiling, and the artist protested: he was primarily a sculptor, he said, and, pointing out that he hadn't worked in fresco since his apprenticeship with Ghirlandaio, he put forward the name of Raphael. This angered Julius, and in the end Michelangelo spent four years perched atop scaffolding engaged in this superhuman enterprise, his face encrusted with paint; he made an amusing caricature of himself in which he is seen standing and straining upward (not crouching, as legend would have it), engaged in executing one of the three hundred figures in this titanic work. He wrote his close friend Giovanni da Pistoia the following satirical sonnet (illustrated with the above-mentioned caricature), using the wonderfully vivid language that was his to command: "I've got myself a goiter from this strain . . . / My beard toward Heaven, I feel the back of my brain / Upon my neck, I grow the breast of a harpy; / My brush, above my neck continually, / Makes it a splendid floor by dripping down . . . / And I am bending like a Syrian bow . . . / Giovanni, come to the rescue / Of my dead painting now, and of my honor; / I'm not in a good place, and I'm no painter." The years passed; he was still shut up in the chapel, and Julius urged haste, even threatening to have him tossed from the scaffolding. These rough tactics paid off, for on October 31, 1512, the work was unveiled, and Michelangelo Buonarroti became in the eyes of everyone and for all eternity the Divine Michelangelo. He was only thirty-seven years old but may have already felt aged, for in letters written a few years later he refers to himself as "an old man," exhausted and fragile, haunted by the idea of death. Which didn't prevent his living just short of ninety years, or his riding horseback and working on the *Rondanini Pietà* until his last days, or his executing shortly before his death a model of the dome of Saint Peter's, which he envisioned as "the sister, larger of course, but in no way more beautiful," of Brunelleschi's dome for the Duomo in Florence, whose beauty he had never forgotten.

garden of the
Villa Gamberaia
Fiesole

"Here I have attained that old-world feeling I used to dream about, a sort of enthusiasm made up of history, mythology, old churches, pictures, statues, vineyards, the Italian sky, dark-eyed peasants, opera-music, Raphael and old Michael. . . . Perhaps I ought to add Henry James. He has been perfectly charming to me for the last three weeks."
— CONSTANCE FENIMORE WOOLSON

THREE CENTURIES LATER, in 1887, Henry James descended from the Villa Brichieri, in the Bellosguardo hills overlooking Florence, to take part in festivities occasioned by the completion of the new facade of the Duomo. He had been invited to the Villa Brichieri by the writer Constance Fenimore Woolson (the grand-niece of Fenimore Cooper), who was ravished by "old Michael"—Michelangelo—and, to a much greater extent, by Henry James, who honored her with an intimate friendship but one whose import was, in the end, cruelly ambiguous. In his letters, he referred to her in such terms as "a deaf and *méticuleuse* old maid" or "a gallant woman" whose "devotion is *sans bornes*," and, somewhat later, as his "excellent" and "distinguished friend." But Fenimore, a sensitive woman of thirty-nine years, nourished hopes of warmer and more binding attachments.

James had just spent some weeks in a hotel room overlooking the Arno, immersing himself in, as he put it, "the queer promiscuous, polyglot (most polyglot in the world) Florentine society," which included an Englishwoman married to a Russian diplomat, a Russian "marquesa" who wrote novels in English under a pseudonym, an Anglo-Italian baroness, an American doctor, and a Scotswoman who performed Italian songs in her villa at Castagnolo. The winter ended, he fled this "vain agitation of particles" and proceeded to Venice, but in the spring, having tired of its "glutinous malodorous damp," he returned to the Tuscan hills.

Thus he once more found himself on the terrace of the Villa Brichieri, whence he could contemplate Florence, the Arno, and, on the horizon, the jagged outline of the Carrara hills, and which he pronounced "the most majestic and at the same time the most *allegro* quarters." It was in this placid and enchanting spot, where he was residing with Fenimore (in spotless virtue, we may assume), that he wrote most of *The Aspern Papers*. In that novella, the Florentine villa becomes an old Venetian palace, and in the pathetic character of the cloistered Tina—she is described as "this high tremulous spinster"—some of Fenimore's features are recognizable. Several years later Fenimore committed suicide in Venice and, among the many annotations in the notebooks she left behind, James would have read the following: "To imagine a man spending his life looking for and waiting for his 'splendid moment'. . . . But the moment never comes." Without the shadow of a doubt, this was the seed from which grew one of the master's own most beautiful works,

"The Beast in the Jungle." It is the story of a man and woman who, having met ten years previous, encounter one another once more. The man lives in constant expectation of some extraordinary event about to befall him, likened to a beast attacking him in the jungle. The woman knows from the start that she herself is the event in question, but he, lost in a world of denial and things unspoken, foils her every play for him. This character, too, owes much to Fenimore, whom James misleadingly designated, in letters written to friends during their cohabitation in the idyllic Bellosguardo hills, as his "neighbor."

"The heat is terrifying, the wine is too strong, the villa is huge."
— DYLAN THOMAS

GIORGIO SOAVI, who lived in Florence just after the war, tells how Dylan Thomas and Stephen Spender, in the city to meet their Italian translator, never managed to see him because he was always sick. When they finally found themselves face-to-face with him, he was installed in his bed, buried under blankets, and could utter only onomatopoeic sounds and frightful groans. The two writers, feeling slightly embarrassed, withdrew, promising to return the next day. Which didn't exactly suit the "ill" man: while an excellent translator, he was quite incapable of articulating three words of English and had resorted to this elaborate subterfuge to save face.

Dylan Thomas spent some time in the Villa Beccaro. And he was right: all Florentine villas are huge, and when it's hot the wine is always too strong. . . . Sumptuous or modest, sometimes extravagant and often stupefyingly beautiful, Tuscan villas, descended from Roman ones, were made fashionable once more by the Medici with, among others, the Poggio and Demidoff villas, La Fernandina, La Petraia (which belonged to Brunelleschi and later received King Emmanuel II), and the villa of Fiesole, where Lorenzo the Magnificent received his artist friends.

Other villas have entertained more ephemeral guests: La Capponcina, in which Gabriele d'Annunzio lived with Eleonora Duse, fifteen servants, ten horses, thirty-eight greyhounds, and two hundred pigeons—until the dreadful day in 1910 when, pursued by his creditors, he was obliged to depart. Villa Miranda, where D. H. Lawrence wrote *Lady Chatterley's Lover,* first published in Florence. Villa I Tatti, occupied beginning in 1900 by the American art historian Bernard Berenson, a walking encyclopedia of Italian lore. La Pietra, long the seat of Harold Acton, the historian and collector who so vividly recounted having heard Diaghilev declaiming Pushkin in the Boboli Gardens—and who once quipped that, if all the wine sold as Chianti were really from that province, it would be as vast as the steppes of central Asia.

And then there is the Villa l'Ombrellino, where Galileo lived.

We cannot neglect to mention Galileo, man of universal knowledge, musician (thanks to his father, who transmitted his own skills to his son), writer, astronomer, physician, the father of modern science, and the object of Inquisitorial persecution—by contrast, the very antithesis of all that is modern.

"To think how I loved the flowers, fields, and sonnets of Petrarch! The specter of my youth rises before me with a shudder."
— ALFRED DE MUSSET

WE CAN'T FAIL TO MENTION Lorenzo de' Medici, known as Lorenzaccio, who, for reasons that remain obscure and to no one's discernible benefit, in 1537 assassinated Duke Alexander, the dissolute tyrant then lording it over Florence. Not that he was especially brilliant, but, as evoked by Musset's pen, brought to life on the stage by Sarah Bernhardt, and realized on the screen by the incomparable Gérard Philipe, he became a formidable romantic hero.

We can't leave out Masaccio, Brunelleschi, and Donatello, who laid the foundations of quattrocento art. Nor Dante and Beatrice, nor Bocaccio, nor Pontormo—who, in a diary entry dated March 15, 1555, noted that he had drawn the arm of a figure in his *Ascension of the Angels,* eaten some fish, some cheese, some figs, some nuts, and three hundred grams (ten and a half ounces) of bread. As for Leonardo, while completing the *Last Supper* he wrote in his precious notebook: "Monday, I bought a piece of cloth 13 lire, 14 soldi ½, the 17th day of October, 1497." And now that we've had more than our fill of quotidian trivialities, here are some figures provided by Giovanni Villani, the meticulous chronicler of Giotto's day: according to him, in 1337 Florence boasted six thousand property owners with sumptuous residences and seventeen thousand beggars.

We ought to mention Vasari, painter, architect, and the zealous biographer of more than a hundred and fifty artists from the past as well as of his own period. He recounts the following anecdote about the young Giotto's apprenticeship to Cimabue: one day, when Cimabue took a break from the face he was painting, Giotto seized the opportunity to paint a fly on its nose. When Cimabue returned to his work, he tried to chase away the fly—which proves two things: that Giotto painted a mean fly and that he wasn't cowed by his superiors. As a matter of fact, in later life he was to make a strong impression—among ordinary people as well as princes and popes—with his sense of humor and his frankness. Worth noting, too, is the adorably roguish face of the happy camel in the *Adoration of the Magi* by the same Giotto.

We should tempt the reader's nostrils with the perfume of the *bistecca alla fiorentina* cooking on chestnut branches and shoots of grapevine. And we ought to escort this same reader through the beautiful city of Lucca, Puccini's birthplace and long the site of a comic book festival: it was there that cartoonist Hugo Pratt discovered that the Tuscans have "an idiosyncratic way of expressing themselves and beautiful asses." We should evoke the fragile *Evening Shadow*, a small bronze that would set Giacometti dreaming, in the Etruscan Museum in Volterra. And the two futurist painters Severini and Soffici, both Tuscans. And Léo Ferré, who lived in Castellina, in Chianti, for many years, and couldn't get over having seen a friend of his who was normally quite reserved—he was a stamp collector!—become a veritable wild beast during the Palio.

We should not neglect to mention the magnificent *Maestà* by Duccio in Siena, nor any of the items marked in the famous Baedeker guidebook with one or two stars, depending on whether they're supposed to excite a degree of admiration that's overwhelming, moderate, or lukewarm—as in the case of the pretty Barberino Val d'Elsa, which doesn't even rate a single star.

"Wretched paintings sometimes give me great joy; with excellent ones often
I can't see why they're excellent. For instance, I love harmonies of blue and
green the way one loves cauliflower and asparagus. Whenever I encounter
these harmonies I'm happy, no matter who the painter is."
— JEAN GIONO, on a visit to Italy

THE SACROSANCT BAEDEKER and Giono's refreshing frankness bring us back to Forster's *A Room with a View,* in which young Lucy enters Santa Croce—the very church that had induced Stendhal's attack—in a state of complete mortification because she is without her Baedeker! As a result, she's totally at sea about the beauties of the building, which at first reminds her of a barn.

"Of course, it contained frescoes by Giotto, in the presence of whose tactile values she was capable of feeling what was proper. But who was to tell her which they were? She walked about disdainfully, unwilling to be enthusiastic over monuments of uncertain authorship or date. There was no one even to tell her which, of all the sepulchral slabs that paved the nave and transepts, was the one that was really beautiful, the one that had been most praised by Mr. Ruskin. *Then the pernicious charm of Italy worked on her, and, instead of acquiring information, she began to be happy.*"

To be happy in Tuscany, without worrying about whether your ravishment is legitimate or not—that is the only reasonable attitude.

THE LAND

HE DEEP VALLEYS of Garfagnana, the pine-forests of Orbetello, the broad melancholy plains of the Maremma, the lunar ridges and ravines of Le Crete near Siena, town-museums and simple villages straight out of medieval paintings—from north to south, from the mountains to the sea, the landscape changes incessantly.

But the Tuscany of one's dreams is to be found in the hills of Chianti, whose oceanic expanse stretches clear to the horizon, punctuated by villas perhaps risen in arrogant defiance of invading armies that are now only phantoms, and by cypress-lined roads so isolated they seem to lead nowhere (though of course it turns out they all *do* lead somewhere). Alternating patches of grape vines and olive trees whose cabalistic forms are kissed by a golden haze in a "humanist" landscape seemingly wrenched from eternity. Perhaps it was here that the idea of an earthly paradise was born, one peaceful day between wars, one morning bathed in raking sunlight, in summertime.

Pages 44–45.
a storm gathers over
a farm
near Volterra

farm
Umbria region

THE LAND

olive trees and haystacks
Tuscan hills

farm
Le Crete area

THE LAND

farmland
near Pienza

landscape
Le Crete, near Siena

THE LAND

landscape
Le Crete, near Siena

THE LAND

farm
northern Tuscany

haying
northern Tuscany

olive tree and haystack
northern Tuscany

haystack
northern Tuscany

THE LAND

farmers haying
Chianti area

SPRINGTIME AND GARDENS

OTTICELLI'S *PRIMAVERA* is one of the most famous paintings in the world. And while Tuscany is beautiful all year round, especially in the fall, it is in spring that this Renaissance ground assumes full splendor. Poppies and mauve irises blend with its tender shades of green; geraniums and roses cling to sculptures that daydream haphazardly along the paths of Italy's most beautiful gardens: that of the Villa Gamberaia in Fiesole, for instance, or the Boboli Gardens in Florence, or the park of the villa Garzoni near Collodi, with its singular array of geometric terraces in ocher and red, its many fountains, and the stairways reflected in them.

Michelangelo once wrote under a design for a window: "If you don't like greenery, then don't come here in May." He was right. And if you're not partial to rain, then you might want to consider September or October, for while spring boasts an angelic visage that bespeaks perpetual renewal, it is also—to be blunt—the rainy season. And when it rains in Tuscany, everyone thinks of the Flood.

Pages 56–57.
a field of poppies
and mustard
Incisa

farm
Le Crete area

SPRINGTIME AND GARDENS

sheep grazing
Le Crete area

*grapevines and
wild mustard
San Gimignano*

SPRINGTIME AND GARDENS

oak tree in a meadow
near Pienza

fields and trees
Piedmont region

landscape with soybean field in the foreground Chianti area

poplars as a windbreak
northern Tuscany

poplars
Piedmont region

sunrise
Rignano sull'Arno

trees
northern Tuscany

vineyards
Chianti area

trees and vineyard
   Torri

Left.
vineyard
Alpi di San Benedetto

Right.
vineyard
Troghi

TREES AND VINEYARDS

83

*vineyard outside
the 13th-century
walled town
Monteriggioni*

85

red grapes
Piedmont region

TREES AND VINEYARDS

white grapes
Porto Ercole

harvesting grapes
Piedmont region

local wine
Piedmont region

TREES AND VINEYARDS

winemaking
Piedmont region

wine cellar
Piedmont region

FLORENCE, SIENA, AND PISA

LUXURY: TUSCANY has three capitals.

Many adore Florence, others find it austere, pretentious, or virile—no compliment when it comes to cities. Its many marvels include Santa Maria del Fiore with its dome by Brunelleschi, the Baptistery, the Palazzo Vecchio, Giotto's Campanile, the Uffizi, the Medici Chapel, Santa Croce, and the Ponte Vecchio. After seeing all that, you can summon up your remaining energy for a climb to San Miniato, whence you can contemplate Florence from above, lost in the warm haze and the silvery gleam of the Arno.

Florence's eternal rival, a city of exaggerated lights and darks traversed by narrow streets converging on the Campo, Siena is a "Venice without water" (Charles Dickens)—a strange image, for Venice without water wouldn't be much of anything. Built entirely of pink and ocher stone that glows softly in the sunlight, it uncaps an unsuspected reservoir of archaic savagery every year during the Palio.

Pisa assembles all its treasures on the Campo dei Miracoli: the Duomo, the Baptistery, the Campo Santo, and the Campanile, or Leaning Tower, which attracts more than 800,000 visitors each year. Until 1990 they could climb to the top, but since then it has been closed to the public, and will remain so for the foreseeable future.

the Campanile (Bell Tower) of Giotto Florence

Pages 90–91. view from the Piazzale Michelangelo Florence

*the Duomo
Florence*

FLORENCE, SIENA, AND PISA

details of the Duomo
Florence

Santa Maria Novella,
a Gothic church
Florence

San Miniato,
a Romanesque church
Florence

Santa Croce,
a neo-Gothic church
Florence

Michelangelo's David,
Piazzale Michelangelo
Florence

Palazzo Vecchio
Florence

FLORENCE, SIENA, AND PISA

bridges spanning the
Arno River
Florence

the Ponte Vecchio
Florence

American cemetery
near Terme di Firenze

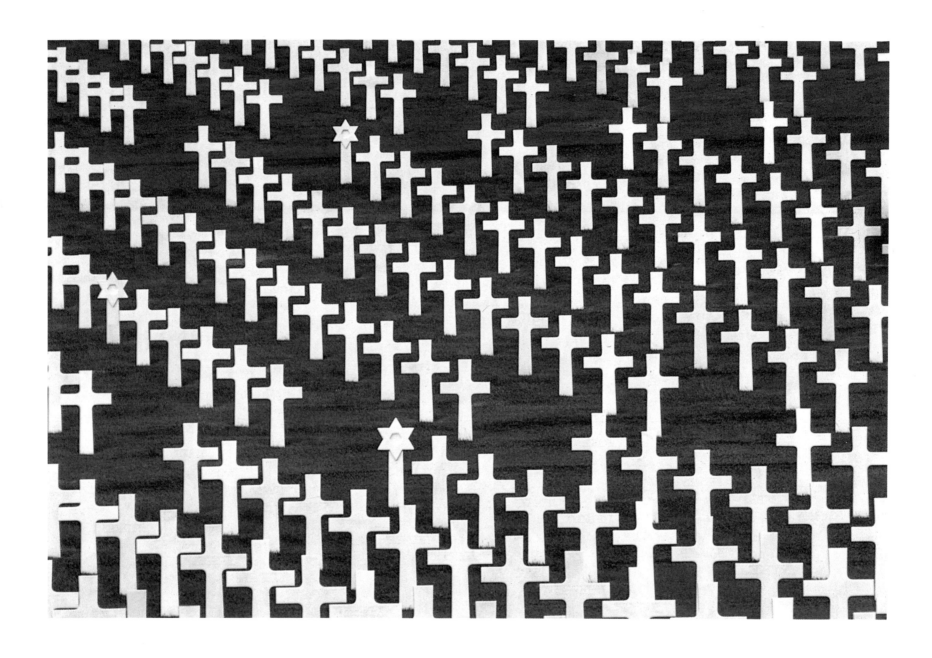

American cemetery
near Terme di Firenze

Overleaf.
Piazza del Campo
Siena

Left.
the Cathedral
Siena

Right.
view of the Cathedral
and the city
Siena

*detail on the portal of
the Cathedral
Siena*

*detail of exterior of the
Palazzo Pubblico
Siena*

rooftops
Siena

view from the tower of
the Cathedral
Siena

Gaia fountain in the
Piazza del Campo
Siena

*wall of the Gaia fountain
in the Piazza del Campo
Siena*

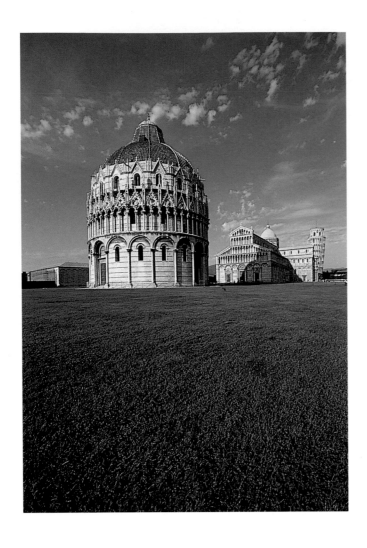

Campo dei Miracoli
Pisa

Campo dei Miracoli
at twilight
Pisa

the Leaning Tower
Pisa

the Baptistery and
the Cathedral
Pisa

the Leaning Tower
Pisa

Left.
Camposanto (cemetery)
Pisa

Right.
a burial plaque on the
floor in the Camposanto
Pisa

view along the Arno
river
Pisa

FACES

 OUNTED IN THE FOUNTAIN at the foot of the Palazzo Vecchio, Ammanati's *Neptune,* supposedly inspired by a drawing by Leonardo, has always been an object of scorn for the Florentines. But it keeps distinguished company. The face of the nymph, executed by one of Ammanati's young collaborators, is infinitely graceful, even when serving as a perch for disrespectful pigeons. Some feet away, Cosimo I de' Medici rides proudly into eternity. The Bacchus on a tortoise at the entrance to the Boboli Gardens is plump, but there's nothing surprising in that: he's the god of wine and the vine—and doubtless of Chianti. Angels and little devils, the disturbing silhouette of Savonarola, the tortured face of Dante Alighieri: the whole history of Tuscany and its beliefs is written in stone and bronze.

Fountain in the Piazza
Santissima Annunziata
Florence

Neptune Fountain,
Piazza della Signoria
Florence

detail on a sarcophagus
of the Pitti Palace
Florence

FACES

court dwarf of Cosimo de' Medici, the Bacchus Fountain Boboli Gardens, Florence

detail of the Duomo
Florence

Medallions on the
Spedale degli Innocenti
by Andrea della Robbia
Florence

FACES

detail on the
Baptistery doors
Florence

Cosimo I on a palazzo
Piazza della Signoria
Florence

Savonarola
Florence

Dante
Florence

Neptune Fountain,
Piazza della Signoria
Florence

detail of
Michelangelo's David,
Piazza della Signoria
Florence

HILLTOWNS AND ABBEYS

RCHITECTURAL SPLENDORS both sacred and profane, peaceful and martial, dot the Tuscan countryside—they give it a rustic, pastoral aura: towns sited on inaccessible rocky cliffs, towers rising into the sky like so many emblems of power and glory, abbeys lost in the greenery. According to legend, the Roman abbey of Sant'Antimo was founded by Charlemagne. That of San Galgano was built on the spot where the impetuous knight Galgano Guidotti wielded his sword for the last time, driving it into a rock before becoming a hermit. Like his contemporary Francis of Assisi, Galgano spoke to animals and was protected by wolves. The nave of his abbey church has long been open to the sky, and nothing is more beautiful than the pink and ocher ruin of this magnificent Gothic vessel abandoned to light and the elements. The honey-colored facade of the church of the Madonna di San Biagio, in Montepulciano, faces the countryside. Pitigliano perches on the summit of a cliff from which rocks sometimes fall—which doesn't seem to bother the cat meditating in the shade in one of the town's tortuous narrow streets. And halfway between Florence and Siena is San Gimignano, called *delle Belle Torri*, with its hallucinatory vision of a proud past frozen in time.

Pages 130–131.
medieval center
Pitigliano

Roman aqueduct
Gubbio

*View of the town and
the Cathedral at sunset
Orvieto*

Detail of Signorelli's
Last Judgment *inside*
the Cathedral
Orvieto

*Outside the same wall,
women sitting on the
steps of the Cathedral
in 1963
Orvieto*

HILLTOWNS AND ABBEYS

*Basilica of San
Francesco
Assisi*

*detail at a cemetery
Assisi*

Madonna di San Biagio
church
Montepulciano

HILLTOWNS AND ABBEYS

medieval walls
Assisi

Castle
Incisa

HILLTOWNS AND ABBEYS

*Abbey
San Antimo*

*fortress
Populonia, the
Maremma*

ruin of the Abbey
San Galgano

ruin of the Abbey
San Galgano

courtyard in the Abbey
San Galgano

towers in the piazza
San Gimignano

HILLTOWNS AND ABBEYS

funeral procession
Volterra

cat in shadow
Pitigliano

horse in barn
Chianti area

late afternoon
Monteriggioni

MARBLE

 ICHELANGELO TRANSPORTED MARBLE from Carrara on ox-drawn carts. His favorite was *statuario,* the white variety used for the *David,* now quite rare. But there are all kinds of marble. *Bianco chiaro ordinario,* used for decoration. *Bardiglio chiaro,* with a grayish tint, and *bardiglio cupo,* which is blue-green. *Paonazzo,* yellow with purple veins, and *arabescato,* light gray with dark gray veins. Then there are *fior di pesco, breccia violetta,* the green marbles of Prato, and the pink ones of Siena and the Maremma.

Mined in quarries resembling glaciers, marble adorns churches and cathedrals, covers entire facades, entwines around columns, combines with brick, provides settings for faces of stone. And its subtle geometry—consisting of arabesques, lozenges, and flowers, of pure whites and abraded blacks, of pale greens and faded pinks—tempers the natural swagger of these monuments with a luminous glow that delights the viewer's soul.

Pages 150–151.
detail, the Duomo
Florence

Above and left.
columns, the Duomo
Lucca

MARBLE

Above and right.
columns, the Duomo
Lucca

MARBLE

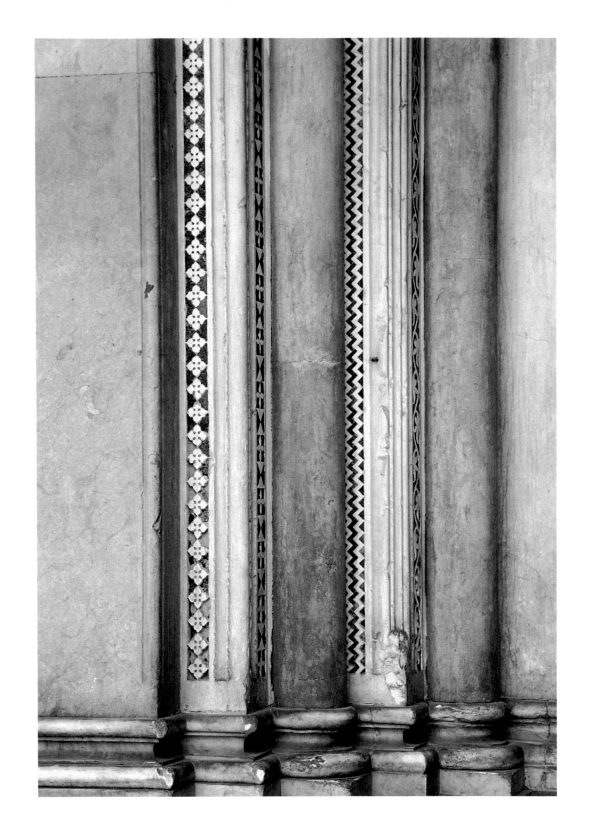

columns, the Duomo
Lucca

MARBLE

*columns, the Duomo
Lucca*

156

Left and above.
block of marble and
view of quarry
Alpi Apuane

Below.
wall detail
Lucca

WINDOWS AND DOORS

 USTERE OR FLASHY, dressed in ochers, greens, or Mediterranean blues, fitted out with geraniums, curtains, or ironwork, the doors and windows keep their secrets. Who are these Tuscans? They're said to be a bit contemptuous, as when they refer to foreigners—Italians and Swedes, for example—as *questi primitivi* ("these primitives"). They're said to be defiant, parsimonious, intuitive, proud, and quite vain of their appearance. "In Milan, the main thing is to dine well; in Florence, to create the impression that one has dined," wrote Stendhal in 1817. They're said to be prone to mockery, sometimes to the point of cruelty, and to delight in public celebrations.

In short, lots of things are said about them, not all of them favorable. The net result is that when you go there yourself you're likely to be pleasantly surprised: you'll find its people extremely kind, straightforward, and warm, ready to indulge your confusing attempt to speak Italian and to come to your aid when you can't finish a sentence.

windows and small openings Volterra

Pages 158–159. windows and doors, Piazza del Campo Siena

priest at window
Pisa

windows
Siena

WINDOWS AND DOORS

windows
Siena

a window of the
Medici Palace
Florence

windows
Florence

window and door
of a barn
Poggio alla Croce

cats on a window ledge
    Gubbio

door
Montepulciano

door
Volterra

door
Gubbio

fresh branches for
brooms on doorstep
Pitigliano

THE COAST

ROM MASSA TO VIAREGGIO, where Byron built a funeral pyre for his friend Shelley, there is now a continuous strip of hotels, pizzerias, discos, and gaudy beach houses. South of Livorno, beyond a few celebrated beaches, is the Maremma, formerly an isolated marsh rank with malaria. The marshes have all but disappeared, and the isolation, too: Principina and Castiglione della Pescaia now offer visitors the charms of their pine groves and small ports. The enormous Uccellina Park resembles a virgin forest, and further south, beyond the Orbetello pinelands, you can take a boat from Porto Santo Stefano to Giglio, a paradisiacal island planted with pines, oaks, and fig trees. The island of Montecristo, long the site of a penitentiary colony from which escape was reputedly impossible, has been declared a natural preserve. But it retains its rocky coastline, which inspired Alexandre Dumas to write the adventures of Edmond Dantès. As for the island of Elba, made famous by Napoleon's nine-month exile there (between his abdication and his escape), it perpetuates his memory by inviting tourists to climb to the top of the cliffs where he meditated and breathe the same air as he did. Pink stone, wind-beaten pines, savage terrain, and magnificent bays: among other beauties, the Tuscan islands offer rocky backdrops of unusual transparency.

Pages 170–171.
*fishermen and cat
along the Riviera
Arenzano*

*Mediterranean scene
Marina di Torre di
Lago Puccini*

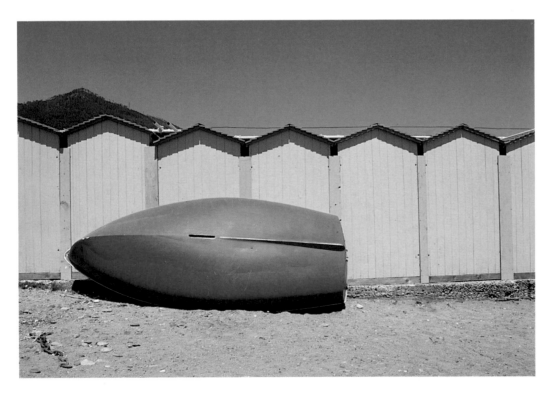

*rowboat
Arenzano*

beach chairs
Marina di Torre di
Lago Puccini

changing rooms
Arenzano

early morning
Cinque Terre

THE COAST

afternoon
Cinque Terre

vineyards along the
Mediterranean Sea
Porto Ercole

sunset
Castiglione della Pescaia

ACKNOWLEDGMENTS

hank you to Bob Abrams for giving us the chance to do Our Tuscany; to Susan Costello for being a terrific editor; to Patricia Fabricant for imaginative design and juxtapositions; to Marie-Ange Guillaume for a text that complements our thinking; to Marike Gauthier for your continued support; and to Myrna Smoot, Lou Bilka, Abigail Asher, and all you nice people at Abbeville.

A very special thank you to our family of friends for understanding the long silences during the making of this book, and to friends at The Image Bank for continued support.

Grazie, grazie to our friends Mario and Diane Modestini for their hospitality and for sharing their lovely Tuscan home with us and to Teresa Galasso and Renzo Raida for all the help and kindness during our stay.

We thank Giovanni and Bianca Gabbrielli for their warm hospitality and for helping us find some special places.

We also want to say "thank you" for much help to: Gino, Rosanna, and Alessandro Martinotti; Nelson Gruppo; Alessandra Marchi Pandolfini; Daniel and Rosalba Elia; Roberto and Mariana Freddi; Agostino Chigi, Porto Ercole; Marion de Jacobert, Uzzano; The Villa Gamberaia; Istituto Europeo (Lingua e Cultura Italiana), Firenze; the ladies of Studio Legale 75, Firenze; Alessandro Saracini, Siena; Lida Landi, Populonia; and the many wonderful people we were privileged to meet in Tuscany.

A portfolio of 20/24 exhibition prints from *Tuscany*, printed with the exclusive EverColor DyePrint process, is available through Moments in Time Ltd. For information and orders, call (800) 533-5050 toll free.

INDEX